theatre babel's

Thebans

Oedipus Jokasta Antigone

by Liz Lochhead
(after Sophocles and Euripides)

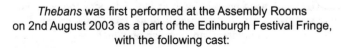

Thebans was first performed at the Assembly Rooms
on 2nd August 2003 as a part of the Edinburgh Festival Fringe,
with the following cast:

Jennifer Black	Jokasta
Peter Collins	Oedipus, Polyneikes
Barrie Hunter	Corinthian, Guard
John Kazek	Kreon
Lucianne McEvoy	Antigone
Bill Murdoch	Theban
Rebecca Rodgers	Ismene
Ian Skewis	Eteokles, Haemon
Vari Sylvester	Tiresias

The original creative team was:

Director/Designer	Graham McLaren
Lighting Designer	Kai Fischer
Sound Designer	Ian Jackson
Production Manager	Mark Ritchie
Stage Manager	Claire Semple
Voice Coach	Carol Ann Crawford
Costume Maker	Ann Matheson
General Manager	Kate Bowen
Producer	Rebecca Rodgers
Administrator	Alexandra Stampler
Financial Administrator	Francesca Howell
Dramaturg	Peter D'Souza
Press and PR	New Century PR
Education Officer	Amy McDonald
Photographer	Douglas McBride

an introduction from
Graham McLaren
artistic director of theatre babel

I wanted to work on Greek tragedy because they are such fundamentally brilliant dramas - even after all the playwriting since, after all the centuries of competition, they stand out. I want to convey what these plays have to say to audiences today, as immediately as possible - to rearticulate ancient Greek drama for a contemporary Scottish audience.

The last time Liz and I collaborated on a piece of Greek theatre was with Medea. It was an unprecedented success, with audiences and critics responding on a profound level to a really remarkable bit of writing.

Not only was the process of creating Medea with Liz a pleasure, the outcome was overwhelmingly good, and I am delighted to be working with her again. With Thebans we tried to build on the lessons we had learnt about Greek drama, and continue to experiment and learn so that we could create something that would move and touch an audience. I hope you enjoy the play.

a note from the playmaker

As I write these notes the Edinburgh Festival Fringe
Programme is just out and I'm squirming to see that Theatre
Babel have credited me with authorship of *Thebans*. Please be
assured that I haven't taken leave of my senses – I do know
that *Oedipus The King*, *Oedipus at Colonus* and *Antigone*,
the so called Theban trilogy, are by Sophocles, that *Seven
against Thebes* is by Aeschylus and *The Phoenician Women*
by Euripides. There is not a single word in *Thebans* that isn't
merely my response to, my version of, something in these
texts in one of the umpteen different translations I read. (I like
unspeakable old Victorian ones with lots and lots of footnotes
on the Greek, myself.)

The conflation, and reduction, into a single play came about for
the specific theatrical task in hand. Some of the things we found
out about our version at any rate of the Greek Chorus in *Medea*,
my last collaboration with this company, invited us to push our
discoveries further. Could we make the core of it all a chorus
of as few as nine actors, our eponymous Thebans, all of whom
would get great solo arias as principals in the drama too, but
would always then return to being part of the team, the choir,
the chorus, the citizens, the ordinary joes? Because I am not a
translator but an adapter I was free to use whatever versions
of the myths seemed to fit our purposes, including Euripides'
unhanged Jokasta, so there's nothing pure or Sophoclean about
this particular telling of the tale, which links *Oedipus* to *Antigone*
with bits of *The Phoenician Women* and fragments of *Seven
Against Thebes*. I am, as ever, enormously grateful to Graham
McLaren of Theatre Babel for giving me the chance to work with
the company on these great plays, and for his patience and
encouragement when I, boringly, predictably, got completely
stuck for a while about how to go about doing it.

Oedipus The King must just be the best play ever written. What
a great story – the King who vows to hunt down the source of
plague and pollution in the land only to discover, much as he
tries to suppress it, tries to not see it till it's more than plain,
irrefutable, that it is none other than he himself. All I've tried to do
is cut it clean to the bone and make the language perfectly plain
and clear. The roles of the messengers in this and the other plays
are, wherever possible, taken over by family members, people

with an axe to grind. We wanted to make it very much the story of one cursed family. And of the powerless suffering citizens under its rule.

It is hard to think of a time in human history when these plays wouldn't seem to be prescient and contemporary, but in our apocalyptic days as, in a great city at the heart of the most powerful empire in the world, towers were razed to the ground, as a new plague spread, as the people of Iraq waited for the overwhelming might of the enemy to be unleashed upon them, as the Palestinians saw that the Israelis would concede nothing to stop the fighting, as a ruler found himself locked into a scenario where he couldn't lose face, as we all waited for a war to begin which we were powerless to stop, it was hard not to feel that the Euripides who wrote Jokasta's great plea to her sons to step back from the brink was, uncannily, writing about and just for us, here, now.

Liz Lochhead, June 2003

information about
Theatre Babel

Theatre Babel's goal is to rearticulate classical drama with a
Scottish voice, lending ownership to these universally great
works for the people of Scotland and beyond.
To achieve this Theatre Babel frequently work with some of
Scotland's best playwrights and poets. The company aims
to create very high quality work that speaks directly to and
about contemporary theatre goers and renders classical work
accessible to a wide range of people.

Theatre Babel's productions have a distinctive style that is
visually powerful and uses minimal sets. Their dramatic oeuvre
ranges from Shakespeare to Moliere to Gogol to ancient Greek
tragedians, and in recent years their work has been seen across
the globe, performing at the World Stage Festival in Canada and
the International Festival of Ancient Greek Drama in Cyprus, and
venues in India, Ireland and the USA.

Their work has received a number of awards including
a Fringe First, the Scottish Saltire Book of the Year Award and
the Dora Mavor Moore prize for best touring production, Toronto.

www.theatrebabel.co.uk

Queen Margaret University College

EDINBURGH

As a part of the development of *Thebans*,
Theatre Babel's creative team worked with students
at Queen Margaret University College in Edinburgh,
and wish to thank them all for their hard work
and contribution to the project:

Cast

Ross Allan
Allan Cross
Maryam Hamidi
Katy Hamilton
Brian Laurie
Russell Loten
Ewan MacDonald
Neil Mackay
Fiona Mackinnon
Victoria MacLeod
Carrie Mancini
David McAlinden
Helen R Modern
Katy Anne Monaghan
Kirstin Murray
Robert Pattison
Cara Jane Roberts
Fraser Stewart
Ingvill Thorkildsen
Andrew Paul Young

Rachel Godding
Robyn Hardy
Sophie Hobday
Ian J Jackson
Gemma Kerr
Geoff Loveday
Curtis Marshall Jr
Kate McSorely
Eve Murray
Anthony Newton
Michael Osbourne
Clair Prime
Katy Rickett
Calder Sibbald
Kathryn Smith
Stephen Smith
Julia Stanton
Rosanna Stone
Craig Walsh

Production Team

Amy Clarey
David Digby
Ella Duncan
Amy Elder

Many thanks to Maggie Kinloch
and Lynne Bains

Theatre Babel would also like to
thank: David Taylor, Ian Smith,
Tom Logan and Roberta Doyle.

THEBANS

Oedipus

Jokasta / Antigone

Liz Lochhead

Characters

CHORUS OF THEBANS

OEDIPUS

KREON

TIRESIAS

JOKASTA

CORINTHIAN

THEBAN

POLYNEIKES

ETEOKLES

HAEMON

ANTIGONE

ISMENE

GUARD

Part One

OEDIPUS

OEDIPUS   my people   Thebans   dear citizens
why   do you come here   waving
banners bearing slogans   with supplications
chanting at the palace gates
protesting   pleading that I
I your King   do something   anything to help
our city in its sore distress?
I am yourKing   your champion
Oedipus   your own
I do not hide behind doors or diplomats
I am here in person   I am listening
oh the man would be heartless who heard
but did not help you

here I am

CHORUS   Oedipus   King Oedipus
here we are   young   old
mothers   fathers   priests
lovers   ordinary folk
all of us suffering   barely containing our panic
waves of it rising in our breasts   how shall we
survive?

for death is everywhere
death blights our crops   they blacken in our
fields
death has ravaged our herds and flocks
the burning pyres of their blebbed and blistered
remains
send up a pall that chokes us
our babies abort themselves unborn
we elders anaesthetise ourselves with alcohol

we youngfolk pervert our lives with poisons
that make false promises to kill our pain
our lovers kiss contagion   one into the other
they wither and dwindle who once upon a time
were strong and sweet and hale
new diseases daily invent themselves
the spores of mutating pestilence
in each polluted gasp of air we breathe

we've prayed to the gods till we are blue in the
                                                    face
and we come to you because you are not a god
Oedipus   but a man Oedipus
Oedipus our King   our liberator
the man who freed us
who by man made logic   or divine inspiration
banished from Theban gates the Sphinx
our scourge the Sphinx
who would have killed us all

the Sphinx who devoured us   despised us
whose great wings beat
whose lion-claws slashed and slit   savaged
who pounced   blotting out the sky above us
whose tail whipped   trailing pestilence
who cackled hatred at us   mocking
her cruel-lovely woman's mouth laughing
you answered her riddle
you outwitted her

and for this famed Oedipus we can never forget
                                                    you
Oedipus our King-elect   our saviour   save us
once more save your children
for without Thebans   what is Thebes?

OEDIPUS   subjects   my children   I suffer with you
            well known to me already is every last thing
                                                    you tell me
            I am not ignorant of
            one item in your long catalogue of grief

if you are sick   if you are suffering
I suffer more

think about it   you sicken singly
you suffer your own private pain
I suffer for the city   and for myself   and for
each one of you

this recitation of your woe is not a wake-up call
to some somnolent and complacent King
the stench of death   believe me   permeates
even the palace
when I paced   insomniac   wracking
my brains for some remedy for my plague-ridden
and sore-beleaguered city
all I could   rationally   come up with this
                                                        time

oh no sooner was it a thought
than I put it in to execution
by sending Kreon   son of Menoikeus   my
                                                wife's brother
my kinsman by marriage   most trusted elder
                                                of this city
to consult the Oracle on our behalf

is there any word or deed by which I   your King
can save our city or protect it?
Oracle   tell us

He sees KREON *approaching.*

OEDIPUS   a gap in the clouds   a chink of light
               let the open eye of the sun shine like a shaft of
                                                        hope

               through this terrible doom
               that so oppresses us!
               Kreon   my kinsman   friend of this city
               what word of the god do you bring back from
                                                        the Oracle?

KREON   on balance   a good word
               for do not even painful processes
               not flinched from but faced and gone through

often lead to sweet and fortunate conclusions?

OEDIPUS   what   precisely   is the message?
your words so far   I must say   make me
neither
unduly relieved   nor utterly apprehensive

KREON   shall I speak out here?   speak publicly?
is it better we talk behind closed doors?

OEDIPUS   here   out loud   Kreon   openly

to be open   to make things known
is my policy   no secrets

KREON   then I will tell you what the god spoke plainly
through the Oracle

we are ordered to drive out
of our city and our state   a pollution
which we have so long nourished amongst us
that it   almost   is too late

OEDIPUS   what is the nature of this evil?
how can we be purified of it?

KREON   by finding and punishing a murderer
who shed unlawful blood

OEDIPUS   whose?

KREON   the blood of Laius the King before you
his death must be avenged
the guilty ones are here in Thebes

OEDIPUS   where was he murdered?   here?

KREON   he left for Delphi and the Oracle
never returned

OEDIPUS   what happened?   are there no witnesses?

KREON   just one
all the King's companions died with him
except one who ran away in terror
he was in such a state all we could get out of him
was that the murderer was
not one but many

> they were set upon by a band of robbers
> that so outnumbered them they had no chance

OEDIPUS   *not one but many*
but how would robbers dare to attack a King?

unless someone here put them up to it

KREON   that's what we thought
but nobody here benefited in any way
and soon we had more to bother us

OEDIPUS   the Sphinx?

KREON   precisely

OEDIPUS   I have to wonder
what went on in this place before I came
it is incredible   you let the trail run cold
no one investigated this appalling crime

till now

as the man who inherited his power
his bed
his wife
I swear to hunt down the killers of Laius as
                                    ruthlessly
as if it had been my own father they'd killed

find this 'sole survivor'

questions must be asked that ought to have
long ago been asked
for Thebes' sake   for the sake of Laius' memory

and for my own
after all   whoever killed King Laius
is likely next to turn his evil hand
against no one else but me

KREON *exits stage and enters into the palace.*

OEDIPUS   people of Thebes
I promise I'll rid this city of the plague

anyone who knows who murdered Laius son of
                                    Labdacus

must speak up now
even if you implicate yourself you mustn't be
                                                afraid

was it some foreigner?

do you know who it was?

if you are hiding something
if you are protecting someone
we will find you out

without shelter
without friends
without gods
this city will spit you out

I'd curse myself with that fate too   or worse
if the murderer were to be found under my roof
and I allowed him shelter there knowing what
he had done

double the agony and desperate suffering of all
                                                Thebes
upon you alone if you won't speak out and save
                                                your city

CHORUS   all I can say is I didn't kill him
              don't know who did

OEDIPUS   then there is no help for this city

ONE OF THE CHORUS
              unless
              Tiresias   the seer?

OEDIPUS   Kreon suggested this
              I've sent for Tiresias twice
              he's still not here

              Enter TIRESIAS.

CHORUS   but here's the prophet now

              uncanny

              he sees everything
              he has the ear of the gods

they reveal themselves to him
nothing goes past him   blind though he is

OEDIPUS   blind Tiresias
you know every secret of heaven and earth
you see what we cannot

this city   only you can save it
help us   tell us what you see

TIRESIAS   it is a curse to know what I know
I know that
I should not have come

OEDIPUS   tell me

TIRESIAS   send me back home now   my lips still
                                                    sealed

OEDIPUS   the only one who can save your city
and you want us to spare you?

TIRESIAS   spare yourself   I beg you
your curses   oaths   and promises have
already made things
that much worse   I won't cap the calamity
by speaking out as well

OEDIPUS   what are you hiding?

TIRESIAS   you don't realize   any of you
the danger you're in

OEDIPUS   I think we're well aware   Tiresias
that things could not be worse
we're dying   all the city
all of us   slowly   of the plague   so speak!

TIRESIAS   I won't   whether I speak out now
or leave without uttering a word   nothing
can alter
what is fated

OEDIPUS   what's fated is exactly what I want to hear
                                                    you fool

TIRESIAS   more harm than good
rant all you want   you won't make me say it

OEDIPUS   because it implicates yourself

TIRESIAS   is that what you think?

well   since you force me   I'll tell you
    this much
the curse you cursed was a curse against yourself
none other   the one responsible for the plague
devouring Thebes is you

OEDIPUS   how dare you?

TIRESIAS   because the truth protects me
you were searching for the murderer of Laius
the search is over
you are the murderer
you killed him   no one else

do you want more?

OEDIPUS   you've already said enough to hang yourself
what else could you say?

TIRESIAS   just this
the woman you married
you committed another crime by marrying her

OEDIPUS   too far   you're dead Tiresias
you blind crippled stupid sightless slave and
    beggar

TIRESIAS   one day soon
men will taunt you with these very words

OEDIPUS   you can't hurt me

TIRESIAS   harm at my hands is not your fate Oedipus
your destiny   your destruction
is in the gift of the gods

OEDIPUS   Kreon   he's behind this
yes   I should have guessed it
my wealth   my crown   his poisoned envy

Kreon   has he been plotting all this time
    behind my back?
he wants my throne

that's it   the one I trusted   loved
comes back from the Oracle with false portents
sends this charlatan   this seller of his soul
who is blind to everything except his own
                                          advantage
to do dirty tricks   and cheap treachery

when did your prophesy save anyone?

TIRESIAS   never   nothing I've ever seen helped
              anyone evade their fate

OEDIPUS   did you see the answer to the Sphinx's riddle?
              who saved the city?   I!
              this man   with no need of altars   birds   or
                                                              omens
              this man saved the city with nothing but his
                                                          native wit
              this man knew the answer   man!
              and this man says
              false seer you have gone too far

              do you know who I am?

TIRESIAS   I do   you don't
              Oedipus you are the man who is the King here
              but I will speak
              you called me slave   I'm nobody's
              not yours   not Kreon's   I'm nobody's
              but the gods'

              I may be blind   but not so blind as you
              you can't see the doom that faces you   I see it!
              you don't know where you live
              or who shares your bed
              you don't know who your parents are
              or how their curse will hunt you out of Thebes
              more surely than an army of invaders
              see your death   do you?
              the most miserable end that any man will ever
                                                          suffer

              this is the day you will be born at last
              and this the day you'll die

OEDIPUS   another riddle

TIRESIAS   solve this one

OEDIPUS   mock all you want   that's the skill
that made me King

TIRESIAS   the criminal is here   now   with me
the stranger to the city who is its native son
the rich man who'll be a beggar with a blind
man's stick
his children's brother and father
his mother's son and lover
his father's son and heir and slayer
see if you can solve that one and it'll drive you
blind

OEDIPUS   treason is your name Kreon
I should have known it!

TIRESIAS *exits.* OEDIPUS *stares angrily after him.*

CHORUS   the word of god comes out of a cave
the earth speaks out   Kreon hears
or mishears   reports it   *distorts it*
is with Oedipus one hundred per cent
or not   sends Tiresias   or sends for him

this was a terrifying prophecy
or misinterpretation
Tiresias is famous for his accuracy
but he's not god is he
perhaps he is malicious
perhaps he is mistaken

out of a cave
or out of a prophet's mouth
the word of god comes
better run   guilty one
fly and you'll not go fast enough
the word is out   the fates and the furies
pursue you now
and Oedipus is their instrument

Enter KREON.

KREON   Thebans what's this?   Oedipus are you
                                             accusing me?
           this is what I heard   it cannot be true
           Oedipus my friend –

OEDIPUS   you traitor

KREON   I'm the betrayed one

OEDIPUS   you killed the last king
           it got you nowhere   I thwarted you
           now you plot to steal my throne

KREON   suspicion   where does it come from?   how?
           listen to me Oedipus then judge

OEDIPUS   judge how an enemy could be nurtured in my
                                             own palace
           in the bosom of my own family

KREON   how   your enemy?

OEDIPUS   don't think I won't punish you like a stranger

KREON   for what?

OEDIPUS   you sent for Tiresias then plotted with him

KREON   plotted   how?

OEDIPUS   when did Laius disappear?

KREON   years ago

OEDIPUS   your Tiresias   was he
           at the prophesying caper then?

KREON   already famous for it throughout the land

OEDIPUS   not a squawk from any of his birds about me *then?*

KREON   not that I heard

OEDIPUS   the murdered King   of course Tiresias was
                                             consulted
           at the time?

KREON   we made enquiries of him –

OEDIPUS	but the famous prophet saw nothing said nothing
KREON	I'm no expert on the ins and outs of prophecy
OEDIPUS	unless he was in your pay and saying exactly what you wanted him to say he'd never have accused me now
KREON	did he say that? if so I'm the one plotted against around here Oedipus did you marry my sister?
OEDIPUS	of course
KREON	and you rule the roost together?
OEDIPUS	we do

KREON	and I'm honoured to be in third place
	I like my life the way it is
	enjoy how everyone knowing I can influence
	                                  things
	takes me into their confidence
	and shakes me by the hand
	why when I've got more than everything I need
	prestige power enough ease
	do you think I'd be mad enough to risk
	                             everything
	for the pressure the anguish the danger
	and the hideous imprisoning
	responsibility of being king?
	
	go to the Oracle
	check if I told you exactly what it said
	
	prove! you won't for I did not but
	prove I conspired with Tiresias then
	execute me at once . as so you should
	
	a dangerous thing to mistake bad men for good
	but even more dangerous
	to falsely accuse your true your loyal friends
	end up friendless

OEDIPUS	so I should wait till this plot succeeds?

KREON   you want me out?

OEDIPUS   I want you dead

               Enter JOKASTA, *she hears* –

KREON   you've listened to nothing –

OEDIPUS   heard far too much

KREON   you're mad

OEDIPUS   you are a traitor

JOKASTA   you're both fools!   have you no shame
               brawling like bairns   the pair of you
                                                over nothing
               while the city is dying

KREON   sister   your husband the king
               has decided banishment's not enough
               he wants me dead

OEDIPUS   Jokasta   your brother the traitor
               would have killed me if he'd got away with it

KREON   in the name of all the gods
               if any of this is true then kill me now

JOKASTA   listen to him Oedipus
               for all our sakes

CHORUS   he swore a solemn oath   your majesty!

JOKASTA   the two men I love most at each other's throats!

               believe him
               in the name of all the gods believe him

CHORUS   King Oedipus please spare his life

OEDIPUS   and lose my own?
               oh   let him go if you say so
               against my better judgment
               I'll *bow to the will of the people*
               we'll see   if we all live to regret it

KREON   you ought to regret already
               that without a scrap of evidence against me
               you were quick to be my judge and jury

OEDIPUS   get out of my sight

KREON   you'll see   King Oedipus

Exit **KREON** *to palace.*

JOKASTA   husband tell me   why   out of the blue
this paranoia   wild accusations
rage at Kreon?

OEDIPUS   wife of my heart   listen
he said I killed Laius

JOKASTA   when did he say this?

OEDIPUS   he used a prophet as a mouthpiece

JOKASTA   a prophet!

Oedipus   my darling
prophets   charlatans every one
or self-deceivers
no one should pay a blind bit of attention
to what these seers say

I'll prove it
a prophet spoke to Laius
note   not the god   his so-called prophet
told him   *one day your own son will kill you*

we had a son
Laius ripped him
not three days old yet   ripped him from my
breast

oh I love him still as if it was yesterday

my husband Laius ripped my baby from my breast
pinned his ankles together and abandoned him
out on the open moor to die
I wept tears and milk – so much for prophecy
the son never killed the father
the opposite horror thanks to that *prophet*

and Laius was killed instead by a band of robbers
at the fork in the road
where the three roads meet

OEDIPUS   where?

JOKASTA   you are white as a sheet
what's the matter?

OEDIPUS   at the fork in the road
where three roads meet
that's where Laius was …?

JOKASTA   so they said

OEDIPUS   what fork?   in what road?

JOKASTA   in Phokis
where the road from Delphi –

OEDIPUS   meets the road from Daulia…?

JOKASTA   yes

OEDIPUS   when?

JOKASTA   a little while before you came

OEDIPUS   oh god what are you doing to me?

JOKASTA   what is wrong?

OEDIPUS   Laius   what did he look like?

JOKASTA   about your height and build

OEDIPUS   oh god   did I just curse myself?

JOKASTA   darling   you are scaring me

OEDIPUS   Jokasta tell me one more thing
was he alone?

JOKASTA   of course not   the royal bodyguard
a small entourage

OEDIPUS   of five…?

JOKASTA   five of them yes   why?

OEDIPUS   who reported it?

JOKASTA   the sole survivor

OEDIPUS   is he still here?   In the royal guard?

JOKASTA   no   he was a countryman from Kithaeron
after the murder his nerves were shot

and – you won't remember this
it was not long after our wedding –
he begged to be sent away back home

it was as if he felt guilty
you don't suppose   Oedipus
that servant had anything to do with Laius' death?

my darling
what's the cause of your distress?

OEDIPUS   my dearest . . . listen . . .
Polybus of Corinth   he is my father
Merope the Queen's my mother
I was the happy prince until . . .
maybe I took it too seriously but
a strange thing   a drunk at a party
made a remark
hinted that I was not my father's son
I was raging inside   held it in though
said nothing
next day questioned them
my father and mother   they were angry
pooh-poohed it   reassured me
I was relieved   but it ate away at me
I kept hearing drunken laughter
and *it's a wise child knows its father*

without a word to anyone
I went to Delphi to consult the oracle
could I get a straight answer to my simple
                                        question?
no   instead a prophecy of unbelievable horror
I was to murder my father
mate with my mother
and sire a brood of bairns
that all the world would recoil from in disgust
                                        and fear

I fled   who could have heard this
and not put so many miles between himself
and his home no star could ever guide him back?
I'll never see Corinth again

or this prophecy fulfilled   I wandered
aimless   homeless   friendless
found myself one day at that place
that fork in the road you talk of . . .
five men   as you describe
some dignitary
who had the nerve to order me
out of the road my boy
in a high-handed manner
the driver shoved me
I shoved back and just as I had
almost
passed them the old man had to
lash out at me   his whip across my face
I saw red   dragged him out
killed him   killed them all

if that was Laius
oh god   I'm cursed
cursed myself not an hour ago
no shelter   no friends
if that was Laius   I'm to be hunted
from the gates of Thebes   if I killed
and sleep in the bed of the man I killed
with that man's wife   touch her
with the hands of his murderer –

out   out   out
where?   not to Corinth
and another curse   kill my father Polybus?
mate with Merope my mother?   I'll die first

JOKASTA   wait Oedipus
             until you hear the witness

OEDIPUS   *not one but many*
             if that's the witness's story
             then I didn't kill him

JOKASTA   that's what he did say
             I heard him   all Thebes heard him

             but the main thing is
             the whole prophecy was wrong

his own son will kill him

Laius' son   my son
a long long time dead

prophets
pay no attention to them

OEDIPUS   get that witness

JOKASTA   he's been sent for
my love go inside and rest and wait

OEDIPUS *glares at her, distracted, then storms inside.*

JOKASTA   I should pray
I will pray though
my lack of faith in prayers will surely
render my prayers useless

do the gods listen?
did they listen when I begged them
to spare my firstborn child
to save him?

will they save my husband Oedipus?
I'll ask them to   I'll pray
I'll pray   I'll offer every last libation   pray
gods save him   gods help him
gods calm his jagged mind
his terrors   his paranoid suspicions
restore his famous judgment gone so raggedly askew
save him from tyrant's pride
restore his reason   give him peace
gods help him

Enter CORINTHIAN MESSENGER.

CORINTHIAN friends
I am a stranger here
I am looking for a man called Oedipus

JOKASTA   I am his wife

CORINTHIAN my lady   all good fortune
to you and your husband

JOKASTA   blessings too   to you stranger
             have you news for us?   from where?

CORINTHIAN   Corinth   good news
             first some bad   but the good news is
             Oedipus has been named King of Corinth

JOKASTA   but his father King Polybus…

CORINTHIAN   alas   is dead

             JOKASTA *starts to laugh. The* CORINTHIAN
             looks on, surprised.

JOKASTA   Oedipus!   Oedipus! come here quickly!

             prophets where are you now!
             so much for oracles
             and suchlike mumbo jumbo!

             Enter OEDIPUS.

OEDIPUS   Jokasta?

JOKASTA   listen to this man
             Oedipus my love

             rejoice
             your father King Polybus is dead

OEDIPUS   how?

CORINTHIAN   of old age   sir
             he collapsed and
             at his age there was no chance…

             OEDIPUS *laughs even louder than his wife,*
             dances her around.

OEDIPUS   dead   dead   dead
             the father I loved so much is dead

             Jokasta
             to hell with all the prophets and their
             birds and omens
             kill my father   did I?
             he is dead and I never laid a finger on him
             unless   after all these years
             he died of missing me!

my father's wrapped up all those predictions
in a parcel and taken them off with him to the
afterworld
where they belong

JOKASTA   my love I told you so

OEDIPUS   I was afraid

JOKASTA   and now there is nothing left
to be afraid of

OEDIPUS   mating with my mother indeed!

JOKASTA   many men have dreamed of such a thing

but they've not done it
it's only a common dream
that's all it is
nothing to worry about...

OEDIPUS   if she were dead too!
I know it is irrational
but I will be   a little afraid
as long as she lives   the mother who bore me

CORINTHIAN   excuse me   sir
interrupting such a   private conversation
but who is it you fear?

OEDIPUS   my mother Queen Merope

CORINTHIAN   but she's not
your mother I mean
not your birth mother   Merope
any more than Polybus
was your biological dad

in that sense Polybus was no more your father
than I was   though
god knows   they loved you like their own

that is why she's sent me here
to bring you back to Corinth as the King

OEDIPUS   never   I can never go back to that place

CORINTHIAN   you were a gift to them
from me

I found you   on Mount Kithaeron

Upset and agitated by that JOKASTA *moves
away from them,* OEDIPUS *and the*
CORINTHIAN *are so engrossed they do not
hear any of her appalled internalised outbursts.*

JOKASTA   no

CORINTHIAN   – yes I was a shepherd in those days
wandered far and wide with my flock
but oh the state of you   just a baby
and your wee ankles…

JOKASTA   no

CORINTHIAN   the bastards had pinned your feet together
it was pitiful   I freed them

OEDIPUS   I've still got the scars

CORINTHIAN   that's how they named you
swollen-foot   your majesty

JOKASTA *and* CORINTHIAN (*simultaneously*)
– Oedipus   – Oedipus!

CORINTHIAN   mind you we don't know who did it
your mother . . . ?

JOKASTA   no

CORINTHIAN   your father?
maybe it was the man who gave me you

OEDIPUS   who was that?

CORINTHIAN   a Theban as it happened   one of Laius' men

OEDIPUS   let me speak to him!   is he still alive?

CORINTHIAN   your people here
would know that a lot better than I do

OEDIPUS   tell me who he is and where to find him?

ONE OF THE CHORUS
isn't he the man you've sent for already?
ask the Queen –

JOKASTA   stop Oedipus   shut up all of you

        Oedipus forget all this   ignore it
        no sense in
        digging up what's past and best forgotten

OEDIPUS   I'm close to finding out who I am and you –

JOKASTA   I beg you Oedipus my love
        go no further or you'll break both our hearts

OEDIPUS   don't want to find out
        you've been sleeping with a bit of rough then
        Queen Jokasta   my sweet snob
        so I might be a slave's son
        or a bastard   doesn't matter
        many a great man's had a humble birth

        or maybe I'm a demi god
        some randy Olympian nailed
        a nymph with a thunderbolt   or came
        in a shower of rain impregnating a servant girl…
        some shepherdess's foot slipped…

JOKASTA   stop   stop   stop

OEDIPUS   I have to know

JOKASTA   if you ever loved me I beg you stop this now

OEDIPUS   I must find out the truth

JOKASTA   you're doomed   my darling
        don't know what you're doing
        lost   lost forever
        no more words I won't
        I'll never ask anything of you again
        no more   nothing   never

        Exit JOKASTA *in great agitation and anguish.*
        OEDIPUS *calls after her.*

OEDIPUS   Jokasta you know me
        you know who I am   the one
        who won't be palmed off with half-truths
        Oedipus the excavator of old secrets

        I will know who and what I am

CHORUS   truth's a great thing

a sore thing sometimes
but a good thing always
always

isn't this the truth about truth?

OEDIPUS   Thebans
I never saw this man in all my life
but isn't this that witness
the man we sent for
coming here at last?

hey Corinthian   is this your man?

CORINTHIAN yes here he is

OEDIPUS   old man   come here
speak up
do you know who I am?

THEBAN   yes sir

OEDIPUS   this man here
is he in any way familiar to you?

THEBAN   no   I don't think so

CORINTHIAN you're joking!
mind it was a long long while ago
but don't tell me you don't remember
those long ago summers we spent with our
flocks on Kithaeron
your flock was twice the size of mine
when it got to the winter
we'd go our separate ways
I'd drive my flock back to Corinth
you'd bring yours back home here to Thebes
is that not right?

THEBAN   if you say so but it was
that long ago my
memory of it's nearly non-existent

CORINTHIAN and do you mind the greeting bairn
you gave me to bring up as my own

THEBAN   (*Agitated.*) what bairn?

CORINTHIAN   because this is the bairn!
                would you believe it
                the King here   Oedipus is none other –

THEBAN   shut up!   a pack of lies   I never

OEDIPUS   calm down Sir
                frankly you sound like you're the liar here

THEBAN   I'm no!

OEDIPUS   are you denying this story about the child

THEBAN   he doesn't know what he's talking about

OEDIPUS   tell the truth   or be made to

THEBAN   I did nothing   I…

OEDIPUS   did you or did you not give
                a child to this Corinthian?

THEBAN   I did   I wish to all the gods
                I'd never set eyes on it   or him

OEDIPUS   so he did get it from you?
                whose son was he   yours?

THEBAN   no   no

OEDIPUS   whose?

THEBAN   somebody else's

OEDIPUS   whose?

THEBAN   don't ask

OEDIPUS   whose?

THEBAN   if I tell you I'll die

OEDIPUS   and
                if I hear you   I think I'll die too
                but you must say it

THEBAN   it was the King's   you must ask the Queen –

OEDIPUS   did she hand him over to you?

THEBAN   not willingly   she
                I took the baby from her arms
                I was only following the King's orders

OEDIPUS	his orders to do what?
THEBAN	to kill it
OEDIPUS	his own child?
THEBAN	he wasnae a bad man sir you see there was the oracle that terrible prophecy about...
OEDIPUS	what?
THEBAN	him growing up to kill his father
OEDIPUS	and why didn't you do what he asked and kill the child? I wish to all the gods you'd obeyed orders
THEBAN	he was greeting sir breaking his heart his riveted ankles and the blood I couldn't I couldnae this man here he had a kind face he came from far away took him far away saved him doomed him if you really are that same bairn I pity you for the gods never did
OEDIPUS	I see it now see everything this wise child knows its father's name at last born at last to the shame of my birth born should never have been killed the one I should never have killed mated with the one – (*A cry.*) Jokasta! got on her bairns who should never have been born I see it all

OEDIPUS *stumbles into the palace. The*
CORINTHIAN *and the* THEBAN *exit in*
opposite directions.

CHORUS	what man can say he's happy? who knows himself? who knows? who can know

what the gods have in store?

high peaks
all the further to fall
who was higher up?
who fell further
into dreadful darkness from the light?

KREON *enters in deep distress.*

KREON   Thebans
dear people of Thebes
with the gods its rulers always

calamity upon calamity for Thebes
and for its royal house

CHORUS   what happened?

KREON   you saw her
my sister the Queen came running in
anguish   grief
I tried to catch hold of her
get some sense out of her
find out what was wrong
Jokasta   sister
what in the name of all the gods – ?
but she tore at herself   her clothes
her hair   screaming she was polluted
not to touch her   ran screaming to her chamber
barred the door   I was battering at it
come out Jokasta   no answer
screaming   screaming   then silence
just one thing I could make out
leave me alone in the name of all the gods
and let me sleep

then he burst in
King Oedipus   my accuser
agitation   he was worse if anything
seized up
Jokasta's shawl from off the floor clutched it
weeping   *Jokasta*
babbling   *my love   never my love*

wife-mother   mother-wife   never
forbidden   taboo-breaker   crop-blighter
plague-maker   babbling
her brooch fell from the torn scarf he wept on
glittered on the ground   he grabbed it
before any of us could stop him
drove the pin of it
again and again and again into his eyes
shouting *I'll be in the dark again* and laughing

blood   blood everywhere
pouring down his cheeks
blood river   pulped mess

Thebans   tell me how a decade of happiness
for my sister and her husband
can in one short afternoon of horror
come to this?

OEDIPUS   open up the palace doors
see for yourselves   roll up!   roll up!

OEDIPUS *staggers on blinded.*

OEDIPUS   roll up people see!
the man who killed his father
fucked his mother   cursed himself
to hell and back again   damned himself
to wander the wilderness
forever exiled in abhorrence from his own city

the horror

what now gods?

KREON   where's my sister?

OEDIPUS   dead
I hope so for her sake

death's too good for me
darkness   my suffering?
if that's what the gods want
then I've plenty of it still to do

KREON   Jokasta!

KREON *rushes back into the palace.*

OEDIPUS   Thebans   my people
               Kreon care for them   my children

               my children my own
               where are you?   love them Kreon
               I'll never feast my eyes on you again
               incest's orphans
               girls you're cursed   who'll have you now?
               boys you're cursed

               I'll stumble   starve
               stones   tares   wilderness
               Mount Kithaeron suckle me mother me
               bury me
               take me inside you
               my mother Mount Kithaeron
               who should have long ago long ago
               loved me to death on your quiet slopes
               I should never have been born
               Mount Kithaeron
               you should have embraced me with stones
               piled them onto me like kisses
               till under a cairn
               lay the corpse of Oedipus non-person
               who never existed

               OEDIPUS *stumbles and gropes towards the
               wilderness. The* CHORUS *watch him.*

CHORUS   Thebans
               fix your eyes on Oedipus
               a blind beggar   our king
               bold brilliant Oedipus who laughed and solved
               the darkest riddle
               saved us from the Sphinx
               enjoyed all greatest fortune
               the man
               everyone loved and envied in equal measure
               there goes Oedipus
               fix your eyes on Oedipus
               drowned now in darkness
               and an overwhelming sea of trouble

look on Oedipus   people
and learn the truth from his sad fate
no man can be ever called happy
till he's made it
happy to his grave

OEDIPUS *is off. The* **CHORUS** *melt away. The
stage is empty.*

Part Two

JOKASTA / ANTIGONE

Ten years later. JOKASTA *enters, stands alone talking*
ironically to the sky.

JOKASTA   old Sun in the sky
you see it all eh?
just shine on regardless
that big bright eye of yours un-
blinking   are you mocking us
or what?   have you no mercy?
don't blush   just   fire up
and set the old ball rolling once again
why not?
another day   another dawn
so snuff every last small star
long long ago   were you watching?
yes   you must have hung there
bold as brass in the bright blue sky
when Cadmus fetched up here from far
Phoenicia
ended up in this cursed spot
one fine day that had the nerve to not
look doomed at all

cocky Cadmus married Aphrodite's daughter and
began all the begats that   via Labdacus' siring
my husband Liaus   Liaus the King
at last was born
and   a good long time after   I
Menoikeus daughter
I am *Jokasta*

married to old man Laius when I was
hardly older than a child myself   this child here

had no children to him
though nightly he battered
at the door of my small shut womb
a barren union
which maddened King Liaus
that what every slave or slut could get
unwanted   he could not have
he went to ask the Oracle: *why won't the gods*
bless me with an heir?
the oracle answered *Lord of Thebes*
land of the fabulous horses
don't bleat on 'bout bairns
isn't an empty pram a blessing when it is fated
that any child you father will kill you
and all your proud house will wade through
                                    blood?
that shut him up   that kept him from my bed
all right   till one night   much drink
                              having been taken and

his lust all fired up
the usual

and I fell

wasn't Laius sorry?
didn't he shit himself as my belly
got rounder than a gourd and still growing
terrified   he was   to think what the god
had warned him of   quite clearly
and how he had offended?
ignoring my screaming   and my bairn's
he tore my newborn from my breast
gave him to a servant to abandon on Mount
                                    Kithaeron
first skewering his ankles together
and slinging him on a stick
in the style of a lamb for the slaughter
that is how he   later   got his name
swollen-foot
that is   in Greek   *Oedipus*

poor shepherds   sometimes   can afford
to be kinder than kings   they couldn't do it
not in cold blood
and you all know the rest of this old story

when the gods' cruel jest showed itself in all its
                                                horror
my shamed husband-son struck out his eyes
                                        with spikes
with the pins of the brooches that fastened my
                                clothes and that he'd
so often undone   but
I was denied the luxury of extravagant gesture
do you not think I wished to die?
I did
I did
but I did not
could not
I had four small helpless children
two little girls   Antigone and Ismene
her father's pet   he named her
and two fine sons   Eteokles and his Mother's
own big strong Polyneikes
I was their mother   so I could not die

The CHORUS *enter exhausted, almost limping.*
One of the CHORUS *ironically sings a soldier's*
rhyme (*to the 'I don't know but I've been told/*
Navy wings are made of gold' rhythm).

ONE OF CHORUS

walks on four legs in the Dawn!
tall on two long legs at noon!
evenin' time he walks on three!
what can this strange creature be?

man   man   man   man

CHORUS   nursery rhymes that soldiers sing   moronic
                                                jingles
might drown the sound of our thudding hearts?

oh that's right   we're terrified

JOKASTA   could-not-die's been doomed to live
            to suffer   to suffer and to see my sons
            raise armies against each other

CHORUS   Polyneikes comes from Argos
            from Argos and a marriage with King Adrastos'
                                                    daughter

            at the head of a great army of Argives
            against the seven-gated walls of Thebes   his
                                                        home

            gods help us!

            the plains are a bristling acreage of men and
                                                    missiles

            Polyneikes comes from Argos
            with kings   generals   strategic
            geniuses   fabled captains
            comes with
            armoury and artillery and legendary battalions
            comes with
            vast armies and advanced weaponry
            stretching further than the eye can see
            against the seven-gated walls of Thebes his home

            and ours
            gods help us!

JOKASTA   Thebans   in my desperation I have brokered
            what I hope will be a truce

            a truce   and talking face to face
            is our only hope of halting this catastrophe
            that seems inevitible and imminent
            may soon annihilate us all

            gods reconcile them   unless you think it's fair
            the same mortals should always be the ones to
                                                    suffer?

            The noise of someone coming and the CHORUS
            shield and hide JOKASTA *as* POLYNEIKES
            enters.

POLYNEIKES the gate was unlocked   as they arranged with
                                                    me

the gate was unguarded   as they arranged
                                    with me
I slipped in easily   but a snare?
you go into it easily   then the trap is sprung
the jaws tighten   the net falls
your blood spills

enemy soil!
my homeland!
I startle at every shadow   my heart is in my
                                    mouth
I fear I won't get out of here alive

my mother   I trust her
and I do not   can not
trust even her

JOKASTA   (*a cry*) son!

POLYNEIKES mother! (*To* CHORUS.) who are you?

CHORUS   Thebans.
            Thebans loyal to this city of the seven towers

POLYNEIKES let my mother go!

CHORUS   who are you   come creeping
            sneaking and skulking among the shadows?

POLYNEIKES Oedipus is my father   son of Laius
            Jokasta   Menoikeus' daughter   is my mother

CHORUS   and we   the Thebans   call you . . . ?

POLYNEIKES Polyneikes!

JOKASTA   your name
            so long since I heard it from your own lips
            an age since I have seen you   son
            let me hold you, let me feel your curls against
            your mother's old cheeks so wet with tears

            Polyneikes   banished by your own brother
            to the shame of all Thebes
            for we did not stop him!

            oh I was scared to death I'd never
            feast my eyes on you again   not in this life and
            here you are!

CHORUS   the immoderate love of mothers for their children!
              gods help them!

POLYNEIKES mother   I was afraid
              but came among my enemies
              foolhardy?   I thought so   but
              couldn't *not* come
              could I choose not to love my native land?
              show me the man who says he does not
              and I'll show you a man who lies

              I was terrified   some trick or
              treachery of my brother could have been
              the death of me *like that*
              so I walked through this   my own city
              the old neighbourhood   the empty streets
              arms drawn and ready   guts clenched
              not daring to breathe   head swivelling at
              every sound
              jumping out of my skin when a scrap of paper
              so much as moved in the wind

              one thing only calmed my jitters
              your promise
              and your guarantee of safe passage
              through this familiar territory
              to the heart of the place that cradled me
              so past the old school   past the shrines
                                                   and altars
              of my ancestral gods
              across the river (its foul-lovely
              river-reek of just-*this*-river
              pungent in the nostrils of this exile)
              taking me back   over the old bridge
              to the cruel shock
              of seeing you so changed   so aged
              so unlike my regal mother
              you!
              drab in black   in rags and mourning
              this tells   mother   how monstrous
              the hell of hatred that splits a family

JOKASTA   the gods are not good!
             did it all begin with that big wrong of your father
             when he married me and made you?
             did it all begin when   in agony
             I gave birth to you?
             I fear it will not end till the annihilation
             of Oedipus and all his house

             glad as I am to see you
             at least the misery of missing you
             let me imagine you were safe   and *somewhere*

             is exile so terrible?

POLYNEIKES   you lose everything

JOKASTA   and keep your life

POLYNEIKES   but you have no voice
             you have to stick the arrogance of who's in
                                                    power
             and swallow it

JOKASTA   I wish you could have swallowed it
             been safe

POLYNEIKES   subjected myself?
             not this mother's son

JOKASTA   don't exiles live in hope?

POLYNEIKES   hope lives in never-never land

             don't get me wrong
             when hope is all you have you live on that
             it's only human

JOKASTA   what else fed you?
             how did you find your daily bread?

POLYNEIKES   sometimes I had enough
             other days I starved   it's simple

JOKASTA   your father's friends . . . surely they'd have
                                                    helped you?

POLYNEIKES   misfortune has no friends
             you can't cook and eat your high-born status

what's rank in another country?
only at home does who we are
have any meaning

home means everything
beyond words   beyond faith
fundamental

JOKASTA   so why flee to Argos?
            what was your plan?

POLYNEIKES my plan was no plan at all but panic
            and to thole whatever next the gods
            would choose to fling at me

JOKASTA   a lucky marriage?

POLYNEIKES none of my doing
            luck?   yes   I fulfilled an oracle King
                                                  Adrastos
            my father-in-law   received once about the
                                                  stranger
            his daughter was fated to marry

JOKASTA   how did you manage to raise an army
            and persuade them to follow you to Thebes?

POLYNEIKES King Adrastos swore an oath he'd restore me
            to my rightful throne   or he'd die trying
            many Myceneans and Danaans march with us
            reluctant but resolved
            a man would be mad to want to go to war
            and the man that marches against his own
                                                  country
            as I do   risks the taunt of traitor
            but I have no choice

            mother   it's an old song but I'll sing it:
            territory   power   wealth   natural
            resources
            are everything
            he who has nothing is nobody

CHORUS   look   here comes Eteokles
            Jokasta   if ever a mother needed all her love

all her passion and persuasion
to reconcile two warring children it is you

gods help us!

ETEOKLES   mother   I've come
as a courtesy to you and you alone
who'll start the ball rolling?
(*Pause.*)
against my better judgment
I take time off my preparations for war
to listen to your arbitration   mother
(*Pause.*)
if no one's for saying anything
I have a lot to do

JOKASTA   wait
impatience does not help or hurry justice
only considered words
commonsense   humanity   kindness
have any hope of unfankling all this
at the eleventh hour and at the very brink of
total war

this isn't some Gorgon you're glaring at
but your own brother
if you look him in the eye you'll speak softer
speak softer and you'll listen better

this is the first and best advice I have to give
to both of you
look each other in the eye
you are brothers
face to face
eye to eye
talk
be true
and keep it to the here and now
forget old grievances
move on

Polyneikes you've come with an army against
your own

claiming you've been wronged
put your case   let's see whether
some god agrees with you

POLYNEIKES truth is a simple thing   no gloss necessary
only lies and injustice need
to be dressed up in fancy arguments
all I wanted was fairness and   frankly
I expected it
so   having lost the toss of the coin   I went
off whistling
into voluntary exile   for one year
I'd be back   I'd take my turn

I must explain to you
in case you have forgotten   Thebans
we had a deal between us
I and Eteokles here
my own twin brother   can you believe it?

Kreon   our uncle
during our childhood   ruled as regent
and well   and fairly
but now we had come of age
it was time for us to take the reins

it was agreed that   turn about   rotating
every year
we'd power-share
this would save our city from any threat
of tyranny or totalitarianism

but here's what happened
he   who swore his solemn oath   reneged
will keep no part of his promise
he won't stand down
he clings to power and keeps hold
of my share in this state

even now I am prepared   on one condition
that I get what's mine   no more no less
to send my army away from Thebes
take power for the duration of no more

than my appointed turn   to transfer it
back to him when my time's up
trust him to have learned his lesson
I will not destroy my own city   or invade it
not unless simple justice is denied me
gods   are you watching?
you know my country has been stolen from me
I know you won't let it happen

this is how it is in plain-speak   mother
irrefutable
surely you know the truth when you hear it?

CHORUS   what this rebel says explains his point of view.
we must say that what he says makes sense to us

is not the man cynical indeed who says
if Polyneikes had the throne
he'd be singing a quite different tune?

ETEOKLES   nothing here is 'irrefutable'
if we all agreed on what was right there'd
be no argument or strife
the facts as I see them are quite different

mother   I'll not pretend that I'd not
do anything   almost anything   for power
now I've got it
I'm good at it   ruling Thebes and Thebans
this half-baked scheme of *sharing*
would have been no good for anybody
now I've got experience I know that

absolute power   oh it would be
nothing short of cowardice to lose that great
good thing
and settle for something less

and what dishonour for Thebes if he should
achieve his aims by coming here team-handed
with an army and a threat to sack his own city!
this is the man who *only has the city's good at
heart*

what disgrace   if for fear of
foreign armies or invasion

I should surrender power to him
if his case was so 'irrefutable' what need had he
of an army to back him up   when reason   he
                      says
can accomplish everything?

he says he'll yield to me after one year
expects me to believe him!
if he did   he'd be such a fool that
that alone ought surely to disqualify him from
                      this office

I'm the honest man here
I say *never* to his demands
now I know that I can rule alone
I'll never be a subject or a slave to him
it won't happen

so I say
come on if you are hard enough   Argive armies
hit us with everything you've got
I'll not part with power
doing the right thing is all very well and good
for anyone who doesn't have the guts
to serve himself just a little bit better than that

CHORUS   powerfully put   morally indefensible
we reject this argument of our Eteokles
might is *not* right   it's madness

JOKASTA   sons   there is more to old age than aches and
                      pains
and grey hairs   experience
grant me this at least if you won't go so far as
credit me with wisdom
(*To* ETEOKLES.)
don't pursue false gods
blind ambition   that's the worst   the wildest
wrecker of human hopes   has been the
                    downfall
of many a family
but you   you're daft for it

(*To* BOTH.)
fairness   that's a more modest god and goal

few men have the good sense to go after this one
fairness alone offers possibility of
forgiveness in families
binds kin to kin   allies city to city
state to state
is how it ought to be but seldom is
for the powerless are always up in arms
against the powerful   hatred has its evil day
                                              again

the night-time and the sun each seize the day
but share it!
neither one is jealous of the other
quibbles when it's ousted
just bides its time and trusts
the natural cycle will return it to its proper place
central to the tides   and in the heavens
holding sway
night and day   that's you two –
but you're *more* different!

kingship
power
who'd want them?
don't mistake them for happiness?
an illusion   power
when they see men suckered by it
the gods start laughing

do you really want to be rich?
that's rich!
wealth brings its wealth of troubles
enough's a richer feast than glut is

Eteokles   what do you want?
to stay in power or to save your city?
what if Polyneikes wins
the Argives overrun us Thebans?
worth it to see your city flattened
turned back to a site of non-existence?
this is after every inch of it has been plundered
looted   polluted

every man and boy been slit from groin to gullet
killed   every woman split and raped
too bad for Thebes if you're too proud
to see how very very possible this is Eteokles

Polyneikes   now you
what were you thinking of?
this *favour* Adrastos does for you   are you mad?
you naive fool!   what possessed you?
suppose   may gods forbid it
you and the Argives conquer
you really think
big Mister Powerful Adrastos will hand over
Thebes to you and go?
the interests of Adrastos are not your interests
are they?   'son-in-law' or not!
could you live with yourself if you
delivered your own country into foreign hands?
could you turn up at the altar of the Theban gods
celebrate your sacrifice of thanksgiving
for Victory Over Thebes?
something to be famous for!

on the other hand   if you are beaten
as I pray to all the gods you will be beaten
how can you go back to Argos?
will your young wife thank you for leaving behind
so many Argive corpses?
perhaps her father   certainly the flower
of their young Argive manhood   dead
all Argos will curse you
thanks to one girl's wedding to a dirty Theban
total destruction and disaster

this   for Thebes and Thebans
even for me your mother   is by far
the lesser of the two evils
but you are facing one of them!

hold your horses   both of you
this is a collision course   one end only

CHORUS   gods save us Thebans

avert the head-on clash of Polyneikes and
Eteokles!

ETEOKLES   get out!   or die!

POLYNEIKES   and who'll kill me?
you?
I'm quaking

ETEOKLES   you should be
look
this hand of mine will send you to hell

POLYNEIKES   but I'll kill you first

ETEOKLES   my brother the dreamer

POLYNEIKES   whose eyes are wide open
sees staring back at him
nothing prettier than naked greed and fear!
you're nothing!

ETEOKLES   you come with all these foreign hordes
to conquer *nothing*?

POLYNEIKES   you're right   I've been over-cautious
a quarter of our force could easily put paid to you

ETEOKLES   you're all mouth!
you've got to trust this truce to save your sorry
life

POLYNEIKES   you need it too   or I'd have you on your knees
for the second and the last time
I demand my proper share

ETEOKLES   demand away!
here's your answer   no
the throne is mine and mine alone

POLYNEIKES   no pretence at fairness?

ETEOKLES   none
now go to hell!

POLYNEIKES   gods –

ETEOKLES   – whose holy altars you come here to lay to
waste!

POLYNEIKES – hear me!

ETEOKLES you think they'll listen to a man who
commits the sacrilege of raising an army
against his own people?

POLYNEIKES you're the impious one
that disobeys all Law and Justice

ETEOKLES the gods of this country despise you!

POLYNEIKES I have been driven from my home –

ETEOKLES – which you would pulverise to dust

POLYNEIKES – unjustly exiled!

ETEOKLES call on the gods of Mycenae   not Thebes
to help you!
I'm not my own country's enemy
you are

POLYNEIKES you banished me and stole everything I'm due

ETEOKLES and now I'll kill you too

POLYNEIKES mother   do you hear him?

ETEOKLES mother?   don't blaspheme!
how dare you call her that?

POLYNEIKES dear city   listen

ETEOKLES get to Argos
call on the polluted waters of the River Lerna!

POLYNEIKES I'm going
but not so far as that
now let me see my sisters

ETEOKLES never!
no sisters of yours   you!   their vilest enemy!

POLYNEIKES mother   goodbye

JOKASTA *good*bye
where's the good pray tell me?

POLYNEIKES this man denies my human rights!

ETEOKLES   because you are less than a dog to Thebes

POLYNEIKES where will you fight?
            by which tower?

ETEOKLES   why?

POLYNEIKES so I'll take position opposite at that gate
            and kill you

ETEOKLES   I'll kill you first

JOKASTA   sons   you are tearing me in two!

POLYNEIKES I'm itching to be bathed in your blood
            as the gods are my witness   always
            now I call on you   my countrymen
            each dumb stone on each inch of this my country
            which I love beyond my life   bear witness too
            I was
            dishonoured   distrusted   disinherited
            driven from you   my only crime   desire for
                                                fairness

            the wish to share
            my one mistake   to trust and love
            this man   my brother
            if I have to kill him first   I swear
            I'll win you back or die   sweet Thebes

ETEOKLES   get   off   my   land

            Exit POLYNEIKES. *His mother* JOKASTA
            *looks after him till he's completely gone, and
            exit* JOKASTA, *weeping, into the palace.*

CHORUS   nothing now can stop it   gods help us
            listen to the silence   ominous
            that will all too soon be filled
            with the hellish clash and clamour of the final
                                                battle

            now here comes Kreon

            useless to remember how happy this land was
            under the moderate regime
            of this elder statesman
            brains   and bright bravery to back it up

vision   a clear path   and he kept to it
no hothead   that caretaker government
took good care
useless to talk in the past tense
useless to say in Kreon's day
Thebes lived in peace

Enter KREON.

KREON   your mother told me
               so it's war?

ETEOKLES   are you surpised?   Uncle Kreon
               we'll win   we must
               our strategies are all in place
               seven good men   the best
               according to your plan and best advice
               brave   with the brains to back it up
               commanding seven steel-hard companies at each
               of the city's seven gates

               our enemies shall not pass

               here goes

               pray gods we'll meet again and I'll deliver up
                                                        to you
               before this city   my brother's corpse
               I promise you
               as you must promise me he'll not be buried here
               on Theban soil   foul pollution
               the stinking and untouchable trash of a traitor
               Thebes' shame

               Kreon if I fail   or fall   though
               our side wins   then also promise this:
               you'll arrange the marriage of Antigone my sister
               to your son Haemon her betrothed   let it be
                                                        today
               let it crown our victory celebrations
               let these lovers and their human happiness
               gladden the heart of all the city for one moment
               before we set to   to count the cost of war

               your oath?

KREON   my oath

now muster every old man still standing
even beardless boys are not exempt
get them   Eteokles   behind our soldiers
you to the first gate   I to the seventh

we can win this   will win this
if gods love Thebes

They salute each other. ETEOKLES *and*
KREON *stride off in opposite directions.*

CHORUS   fear   that's the god that rules us now
our hammering hearts won't stop
a tiny pulse of agitation beats behind every
                                             temple
little incendiaries of anxieties ignite
till fullblown terror catches fire and overwhelms
                                             us
we are quaking

any moment now the noise of battle
loud alarms and sirens
drowned out in louder clash and screaming
our city's finest   our bravest men
are on the very battlements

what will happen to us all
to our prayers and our hopes?
from the enemy skies a hail of missiles
comes whistling down   raining on us
                                             bullseyes
targeting our defenders with terrifying accuracy

cities stand so tall
we live in them forgetting they can be broken
brought down in flaking ashes   smoke and
                                             horror

the broken city is a forest that offers no shelter
no shelter for the   screaming baby
starving on the breast of the murdered mother
for the raped girl splayed beneath the laughing
                                             soldiers

for the old men herded like beasts
for their mutilated corpses
for the old women dragged by the hair like
                                    animals
for the skulls cracked like egg-shell

now is the time
time for our terror that has been so long growing
to be harvested
nightmare may be tomorrow's news
but at least   at last
for good   for ill
the battle will be over

those among us who are men
or remnants of men   must fight
adrenalin and terror   a tidal wave
sweeps each to a fateful city gate

and those who are women
must cower at home and pray and wait

*Smoke? Noise? Sirens? A battle and a passage
of time have been represented by this last*
CHORUS *and this noise. Silence. And
immediately onto the empty stage through
smoke runs a lone figure, battle-stained,
exhausted in common soldier's uniform,*
HAEMON.

HAEMON   is any one there?   I must see Queen Jokasta

             HAEMON *batters at gates of palace.*

CHORUS   after all the noise and clash of battle
             silence   then
             one man batters at the palace door

             HAEMON *batters at palace gates again.*

HAEMON   Jokasta   I have news for you

             JOKASTA *comes out of the palace.*

JOKASTA   Haemon
             so Etokles is dead?

HAEMON   why do you say so?

JOKASTA   you come to me   his cousin   his captain
the man who's marched by his side always
I must know: is Eteokles my son
dead or alive?

HAEMON   alive

JOKASTA   the city walls?   the seven towers?

HAEMON   safe as houses   unbreached
calm your fears   it was touch and go
but our city is not taken

JOKASTA   tell me one thing and swear you tell the truth:
is Polyneikes still alive?

HAEMON   the pair of them   alive
there are piles of dead on both sides
heaps and heaps of them
but both your sons are still alive

JOKASTA   what else do you have to tell me?

HAEMON   perhaps I should stop
while all the news is good

JOKASTA   what else?

HAEMON   I came to tell you this
but now the time has come I do not want to
let me go Aunt   Eteokles needs me

JOKASTA   tell me   don't leave me in the dark

HAEMON   your sons are going to fight
hand to hand in single combat to the death

A cry from JOKASTA. *Then she batters the door.*

JOKASTA   Antigone!

HAEMON   they spoke words that never should have been
spoken!
Eteokles started it
shouting down from the tower
commanders of the Argive armies

Thebans   every man left standing
don't for Polyneikes' sake   or mine
further gamble with your lives
one to one   my brother and I
I dare him   to the death
this world is not big enough for both of us
if I win Thebes is mine   go home
if he kills me it's his   all his
but look   I'm not exactly quaking

up jumped Polyneikes from the ranks
you're on!
and from the Argive ranks a cheer went up
then from the Theban side
a huge jeering ululation of approval

on these terms the truce was made
commanders in the middle ground
took oaths   made terms of treaty
that Eteokles   Polyneikes
whoever wins   and lives
wins everything

stop them Queen Jokasta from this disastrous
                                                    fight

ANTIGONE *comes on in wedding dress, hem*
half pinned up.

ANTIGONE   mother?

She sees HAEMON *and runs to him with a cry*
of joy. They embrace passionately.

ANTIGONE   Haemon!

JOKASTA   your brothers' lives are lost

ANTIGONE   both my brothers   dead?

JOKASTA   as good as   they have decided to fight
                   hand to hand

ANTIGONE   what are you telling me?

JOKASTA   nothing good

                    hand to hand   one to one
                    and to the death
                    come with me

ANTIGONE   where?

JOKASTA   you have to stop your brothers' feud

ANTIGONE   how?

JOKASTA   somehow!
            on our knees   we'll pray
            and plead with them
            (*To* HAEMON.)
            take us to that place
            (*To* ANTIGONE.)
            and if we fail I'll die with them I swear

            HAEMON, ANTIGONE *and* JOKASTA *exit*
            fast.

CHORUS   men fighting hand to hand
            brother fighting brother to the death
            this is a bad dream we've had
            since we were children

            we are descendants of the sown men
            Thebans born of the race that sprung up fighting
            sprouting armed   awake   and angry
            from the soil   when Cadmus killed the serpent
            sowed the serpent's teeth

            these were the lullabies they shushed us with

            Cadmus founder of Thebes
            Cadmus one of the four brothers of Europa
            that fabled child
            yes   the white bull stole sweet Europa
            swimming with her out to sea
            to the shouts of her astonished brothers

            aye Cadmus founder of Thebes who
            obeyed the god killed the serpent
            sowed the teeth   and threw the stone
            among the sown men spreading discord
            manmade discord made them fight

hand to hand   one on one   brother
                                                    to brother
annihilating one other

clash of combat   steel on steel   clanging
                                                    shields
hacked limbs   blood river   blood swamp
blood torrent   butchery

these were the lullabies they shushed us with

Eteokles and Polyneikes
descendents of the sown men
fighting to the death
two fated figures locked in combat   our
Theban emblem

ISMENE *comes out of the palace.*

ISMENE   where is everyone
where has my mother gone?
where's Antigone?   my sister
if Thebes has victory
this is your wedding day

if Thebes has victory
why does my uncle come
so stooped   a weight of pain
under a cloud of grief that's palpable –
Kreon!

KREON *comes with* JOKASTA's *dress,*
blooded, folded.

KREON   Ismene the news I bring is terrible

ISMENE   so tell it

KREON   your brothers are dead   there's more

ISMENE   tell it   `   two dead of one catastrophe

KREON   your mother died with her sons

A terrible cry from ISMENE.

CHORUS   cry out
lamentation is your name Ismene

ISMENE   tell me what happened   I must know

KREON   your brothers put on their armour
stood between two armies
two brothers   two commanders
glinting   one against one
hellbent on combat   each praying to his god
he'd bathe himself from head to foot
in brother's blood

ISMENE   are you saying they killed each other?

KREON   a bloody clash   an even match
we sweated it out just watching them
while with their expert shields they parried
time on time   beyond exhaustion
blow on useless brilliant blow   but
one stumble   one thrust
a retaliation   they wounded one another
                                          mortally

CHORUS   cursed Oedipus
the curse you cursed your sons with is fulfilled

KREON   this is not yet the worst bit
just in time to see them fallen in their blood
to hear the deathrattle in her children's throats
your mother and Antigone arrive
gasping   pell mell   in extremis
the cry that came from out your mother
must have melted even Argive hearts
even as it chilled me to the bone
my sons   my sons
too late to help you   falling on them keening
lamenting that she'd ever given suck

Antigone your sister
berated them as they lay bleeding
my mother's keepers in her old age!
my wedding-wreckers   oh my beloved brothers
Eteokles   dying   heard your mother
put out a pale hand to her
and though he could not speak   his eyes spoke
love and grief and gladness he had what

all men dying in battle crave at last
their mother's arms
this other   he was still alive
and looking at his sister and his old broken

mother

used his dying breath to speak
we are finished   I pity you
my mother   my sisters   even my dead

brother

I killed and who killed me
my dearest   my direst enemy
my brother always
he gasped   harsh   it rattled
he was fading
the fittest thing you who brought me to the world
should put me in the earth so
take me Mother and sister
I shall have as much inheritance as
my father's curse promised me I'd win
and that (he tried to laugh)
'only by bloodshed
Theban soil   enough to bury me'

he'll see!   he died   they died together
your two brothers

A cry from ISMENE.

KREON   not the worst yet   listen
your mother snatched up some sword
that lay there among the mangled corpses
and through her own soft throat
she thrust the steel
she lies dead   her loving arms outflung
between the two dear sons
who caused her so much grief

A cry from ISMENE.

KREON   now each side sprung fresh to arms
their side claiming   Polyneikes
struck first blow and he had won
ours that   since they both were dead
irony indeed to credit victory to either

violent strife broke out again like wildfire
but this time we took the initiative and won

the plains are black with Argive army in full flight
they've run   except those that are going

nowhere

there are stinking piles on piles of those

we've not escaped this carnage either
tonight many Theban homes will weep
just as loudly as others will be rejoicing

Enter ANTIGONE *with* HAEMON – *each of
them with a folded blooded garment.*

KREON   time for a respite from tears
before more tears   while we
arrange fit and due and honourable burials

dear sister   poor Jokasta
you bore so much and lived
after a life so full of horror this mother's grief
was one grief too many

they'll bear her to the palace
and Eteokles must be carried home
honour him   a Theban hero

KREON *rips* POLYNEIKES' *garment from
ANTIGONE, tears it and spits on it.*

KREON   this other   this pollution I'll not name
because the sound would soil my tongue to even

utter it

this carrion   this worse than animal
who came to attack his home   his own
our Thebes   let them take *this*
the birds of prey may pick it over to their hearts

content

may his bare butchered stinking corpse
be mauled and mangled
torn apart and squabbled over by rude dogs
Thebans   take *this*
well away beyond our walls and borders
dump it on some midden like the dung it is

and make public proclamation to all Thebans
this is what happens to traitors
anyone caught crowning this corpse with herbs
or sweet libations   anyone placing *this* into
                                    the earth
does so under pain of death

Antigone   go in   go on   take your sister
you must mourn your mother and your only
                                    brother
then get ready for first a funeral then a feast
when you will marry Haemon

Thebans   dear people   we have paid in
                                    blood
the gods indeed   this happy day
delivered us from defeat   from disaster

Thebans you've been loyal
many of you since Laius's day
loyal through the reign of Oedipus
through my regency till the two princes came of
                                    age
loyal to Eteokles who now lies dead
a hero   and as I assume the throne
as must   for who else remains to rule in
Thebes?
I ask you to be loyal still

first let me be quite clear
I've no time for the man
who bends with the wind
who sacrifices principles for popularity
this is who I am
and I will rule justly   you shall see

the enemy of this city is my enemy
the enemy of Theban gods is my enemy

and that is why   my people
this traitor Polyniekes   must be left to rot
a warning to all the enemies of Thebes

place guards   ensure
no-one touches the body

he who does will die and suffer the same sorry
                         stinking fate

this is my decree
I will never   can never change it

CHORUS   whatever   great Kreon   you decree
                no man will dare to disobey

Exit KREON, *leaving* ANTIGONE, HAEMON
and ISMENE *alone.*

ANTIGONE   no shame
                no pain   no anguish of grief
                but the gods will put us through it

HAEMON   Antigone   my love
                come in   you heard my father
                no help for all this grief
                except you let me make you happy

ANTIGONE   go Haemon   wash the battle off
                get ready for this wedding

HAEMON   come

ANTIGONE   soon
                go   or else I'll never come
                sister stay

Her intensity wins the day. HAEMON *goes off
but very, very reluctantly, looking back. The
moment he's gone –*

ANTIGONE   choose Ismene!

ISMENE   choose what?

ANTIGONE   to help me   or to not-help

ISMENE   do what?

ANTIGONE   bury our brother

ISMENE   against the law

ANTIGONE   – your brother!   vulture meat
                I won't betray him Ismene
                will you?

ISMENE   think
                think Antigone
                think of our father   the father we loved
                hated
                shamed
                tearing his eyes out in agony

                think of our father's lonely death
                a weary wanderer in far Kolonos

                think of our mother slashing her own throat
                her mother's heart broken in her by our brutal
                                        brothers
                our brothers who murdered each other
                all in the hellish conflagration of this one single
                                  searing day

                only we two are left Antigone
                we are only women
                do you want us to be next to die?
                must we keep it going   this curse?

                I hope the dead will forgive us
                for it is suicide
                to fight with Kreon

ANTIGONE   I asked you sister   I won't ask again
                even if you begged
                I wouldn't let you help me now

                I will bury him   I Antigone
                his sister   happy to die for it
                to lay my loving body next to his sweet corpse

                it's the dead we should placate Ismene
                we'll be a lot longer dead than we are alive

                deny the dead their dues by all means Ismene
                the gods won't forget

ISMENE   I'd never scorn the gods
                but I can't fight the king   can't fight the law

ANTIGONE   I'm going to bury my brother

ISMENE   I'm so afraid for you

ANTIGONE   don't be   fear for yourself

ISMENE   at least
keep it secret   I'll stay silent too

ANTIGONE   secret!   tell the whole world   shout it
or I will hate you even more

ISMENE   what you want to do is just impossible

ANTIGONE   don't let the dead hear you say *impossible* and
hate you
It is *imperative*   I won't stop while I have
breath in me
or last scrap of strength to follow this through
until the end

danger and death are not dishonour

Exit ANTIGONE, *determined, after her.*

ISMENE   remember   whatever happens
I will still love you   always

ISMENE, *weeping, goes very slowly towards
the palace.*

CHORUS   we ought to be singing of victory
today we won a victory
at great cost   a great victory
but   the ominous words of Antigone
the tears of Ismene   fill us with
foreboding

And as she does, enter KREON *from the palace.
He sees the terribly distressed state she's in, is
moved, goes to try and reach out.*

KREON   Ismene   niece my dearest –

ISMENE   please uncle let me be

*She exits into the palace very quickly, avoiding
him.*

KREON   these two poor orphaned girls know they have
a new father in me   as Thebes has
a new father in me
believe it

Thebans: Eteokles lies in state
we will bury him a Theban hero
Jokasta my dear sister lies embalmed
her maidservants have clothed her for burial
dressed her hair   they weep for her

mothers weep for her
as now Ismene her own daughter weeps
where is Antigone?
have you seen her?

CHORUS   we saw her running
saw her wearing her bridal dress
are we foolish to hope she's seeking Haemon?
surely she's seeking Haemon
your son   her bridegroom?
surely Haemon will turn her heart towards a
happy future?

GUARD *enters. He's very nervous.*

GUARD   Sir
sorry Sir   I'm sorry
Sir   I wouldnae want you to think that . . .
Sir listen
Sir I know I could have   mibbe should have
but naw
aye   well thing is . . .
I know I'm sweatin so I am
cannae get a breath
but that's no because I've been running
because I've no been
I've been walking very slowly
two steps furrit   wan step back   humming
                                                          and hawing
fact I vernear turned back
vernear did a runner
dithering and swithering wi masel
are you daft?
what are you going to say?
what's he going to say when you say it?

then I thought to myself I thought   naw

I've got to go   I better
say he hears it from somebody else
be so much the worse for you son
so it will

KREON   what are you talking about?

GUARD   that's why I thought I'd never get here
back and furrit   *aye   naw*
go don't go   speak oot   shuttit
thing is I suppose what's gonnae happen's
gonnae happen
fate   it's all one   intit?
what's for you willnae go by you, eh?

KREON   speak

GUARD   before I start Sir I've got to say something
and I hope you'll hear me   bear with me Sir
but it wasnae me   be very clear about that Sir
I'm no to blame

KREON   I'll blame you all right if you don't stop
blethering

GUARD   thing is I wouldnae want you to think –

KREON   in the name of all the gods
say what you have to say then go to hell

GUARD   alright I'll just say it
the corpse Sir   somebody's buried it

KREON   what?

GUARD   well
sortae covered the body with a wee sprinkle of
stour really
but beside it are laid out the usual sortae
funeral libations…

KREON   who would have dared…?

GUARD   it wasnae me that's all I know
see the grunns hard as iron so it is
there's no a mark of a spade or a rake
or even a scrape left by a trowel
there's nae footprints

KREON   no clue?

GUARD   nane

KREON   who found out what had happened?

GUARD   when we changed the guard
             one of the boys noticed   shouted on me
             there it was   covered
             no covered ower properly
             jist sortae   as if it was to save it
             from the shame of an unburied corpse

KREON   surely it must it have been some animal?

GUARD   naw   nae dogs nor nuthin had been at the body
             gods you should have heard the carry on when
                                            we funn it
             wan guard blaming the ither
             everybody shouting and bawling at everybody else

             we were all   *I'm gonnae walk through fire so*
                                            I am
             I'll grab this rid hoat iron and sweer by all the
                                            gods
             I hud nothing to dae with it
             and I'm no in-the-know either so don't suggest it

             it might have all ended up in a fight
             if somebody hadnae scared the shite oot o us
             shut us up sharp by saying
             listen   who is gonnae tell Kreon?

             we knew if we kept schtum and said nothing
             we would all be in for it
             so we drew for it   didn't we?
             and lucky old me got the short straw so here I am
             and naebody likes the bearer of bad –

KREON   who would have dared?

CHORUS   Kreon our King   perhaps some god –

KREON   Thebans   don't be foolish please

             of course it was the gods wanted that body
                                            honoured

saviour of Thebes!
yes the gods respect that rebel   adore that
                traitor   that terrorist
I don't think so

from the word go
there have been those   yes people in this city
                      Thebans
out to undermine me
there are mutterings   they plot against me
the opposition   that's who it'll be
they'll be responsible   will have bribed
some lowlife scum to cover the corpse and
make a pathetic little point
about what they think of me and of my edicts
money   nothing some folk won't do for it

but they are not going to get away with this
guard!   you!

GUARD   Sir!   It wasnae me sir

KREON   find him   you fool   and bring him here to me
the one among the guard who took that bribe
or I'll hold you   and you alone   responsible

Exit KREON *into palace. Once he's out of
earshot* GUARD *shouts.*

GUARD   ach   we can only hope the criminals decide to
show up well!
tell you one thing straight
whether they dae or whether they dinnae
you'll no see me for dust
I'll no be back   no chance

luckier than I expectit to get oot alive this time
and I'm going to risk it again?

aye   I look that daft

GUARD *exits quickly.* KREON *reenters, stands
thinking while –*

CHORUS   we are the one animal which knows it is going
                      to die

we are the one animal which buries its dead
honours the single life which is over
grieves over our own oncoming death
in honouring the unique human life which is
                                        now over

humankind?
fore-knowledge of our inevitable deaths
and reason

reason is ours
dilemmas perplex us
if we do this thing that
if we do that thing this
reason is ours
we can come to just decisions
reason is ours

we can change our minds with changing
circumstances –

Guard enters with ANTIGONE.

CHORUS   O gods no
            please don't let it be Antigone
            Antigone
            Antigone
            have you dared to disobey?
            been mad enough to cause your own death now?

GUARD   we've got her   caught her red-handed
            where's Kreon?

CHORUS   King Kreon?   here he is

KREON   what's this?

GUARD   Sir   to be honest with you
            when I left here before
            I thought to myself wild horses couldnae drag
                                        me back
            but never say never eh?
            here she's   ask her
            she'll have to admit she is the guilty one

KREON   where did you find her?

GUARD   burying the body   caught in the act

KREON   how?

GUARD   It wis like this: I'm away back   my heid
                                                 still nipping
           wi all the threats you'd heaped upon me
           shitting masel I wis   and I tellt the rest of
                                                          them
           so we set to and swept the stour off the corpse
           chucked away the offerings
           scraped the earth off it with our bare haunds
           but the smell
           gods!   the flies   the buzzin
           the stench would have knocked you out so it
                                                          would

           so we stood a bit further away
           up wind in fact
           but where we could still see the corpse
           see it perfectly
           no chance of another fiasco   no way
           no laxness   no taking it easy and nae forty
                                                          winks
           wan at a time   we would keep watch

KREON   and you saw…?

GUARD   aye   I'm getting to that bit
           coorse just my luck   I'm up first   fine
           first while fine   nothing happens
           midday the heat gets worse
           blazing doon it wis
           and a great dust storm blaws up
           a whirlwind   unbelievable

           the leaves ripped off the trees
           you'd to shut your eyes and just thole it
           eventually it's all over and that's when we see her
           screaming like a banshee   like a bird that's
           come back to its nest and funn it herried
           cursing whoever had cleaned the corpse off
           there she is digging away with her bare hands
           covering the body with dirt again

oot there in broad daylight
no caring at all who saw her

when I ran to catch her
did she stop?
did she hell
just went on replacing the offerings
in a deliberate and ritual kind of a fashion
as if I wasn't even there

when I grabbed her
she bit me and tried to keep on digging

so
sorry I'm sure it's just a lassie no some great plot
and sorry for the lassie
almost as sorry as I'm gled to be in the clear
masel

KREON   enough!
Antigone   look at me
is this true?

ANTIGONE   yes

KREON   Antigone
you knew   tell me you did not understand
that I had forbidden it when you buried this body

ANTIGONE   yes I knew   of course I knew
you made yourself very clear   Uncle Kreon

KREON   it was decided by your only brother Eteokles
I promised him

ANTIGONE   a promise to do a wrong thing isn't binding

KREON   admit it was only right to throw it to the dogs

ANTIGONE   no   neither lawful nor just

KREON   yes   a traitor to his own

ANTIGONE   and for that
he paid the penalty of the gods already
his death
death for the wrong of seeking his rights?

KREON   you heard me yet you still dared to disobey

ANTIGONE   yes   I had to
                    it wasn't the law of the gods or of the dead
                    it was   nothing to me

                    I obey eternal laws

                    oh I knew full well that I would die for it
                    I will die one day with or without your law
                    or you proclaiming it and the sooner the better
                    a sweet blessing when it does come   death
                    how could it not be?   I'll bear it

                    the only unbearable thing
                    was to leave my brother   my mother's son
                    rotting   unburied

                    you think me a fool for
                    honouring the eternal dead
                    and breaking the foolish foolish law
                    of an impious mortal fool?

                    tell me
                    which of the gods have I offended?
                    what god's law have I broken?

                    none
                    Kreon's law   not any god's
                    if Kreon is right   gods punish me now

                    but if he is wrong
                    gods punish and scourge this sacrilege called
                                                              Kreon

CHORUS   she is her father's daughter
                    the children of Oedipus are cursed
                    with never knowing when to stop

KREON   she'll stop   the hardest iron is the first to snap
                    the proudest horse gets bridled and gets broken
                    it is her pride that will kill her
                    that pride she showed when she broke my law
                    the pride she shows now as she brags about it

                    I will not tolerate it

CHORUS   Kreon our King   your own niece

KREON   were she my own daughter I'd still exact the
                                                            penalty

            get her sister
            bring Ismene to me now

            GUARD *goes in to fetch* ISMENE.

            I saw her   weeping
            as mad as her sister that one
            weeping and wailing and wringing her hands
            she shrank away from me like a guilty one
            so stupid they give themselves away
            these sisters
            they will both be punished for what they have
                                                            done

ANTIGONE   the penalty is my death
            surely that'll satisfy you?

KREON   it will

ANTIGONE   what are you waiting for
            kill me now   at once
            go on
            nothing more to be said Kreon
            I did that glorious thing   I buried my brother

            the right thing   all the people of this city
            agree with me
            these Thebans here would cry out and tell you so
            if they weren't so cravenly afraid of you

KREON   you're wrong   a lone voice Antigone

ANTIGONE   they all know exactly what is right
            but are too cowed to tell you

KREON   not so   you shame yourself

ANTIGONE   shame myself honouring my own brother?

KREON   and Eteokles   was he not your brother too?

ANTIGONE   he was

KREON   and you insult him   honouring his murderer

ANTIGONE   that's not what he would think

KREON   exactly what he thought   I promised him

ANTIGONE   alive he thought that   perhaps
but the dead are not enemies
the dead are brothers

how can I love one and hate the other?
I love them both

KREON   then love them
away to hell then and love them there
I will not be told what's what by a silly little girl

CHORUS   here comes Ismene   Kreon
in tears for her sister

Enter ISMENE *with the* GUARD *guarding her.*

KREON   two traitors in my own   my closest family
tell me: did you or did you not have a hand in
this?

ISMENE   I helped her   I must share the blame

ANTIGONE   no   she did not help me   did nothing
you refused Ismene   you can't share the
glory now

ISMENE   I was too scared   but now I want to be with you
to the death Antigone

ANTIGONE   too late Ismene   too late
our dear dead brothers saw me act alone
they know   love isn't words   it's action

ISMENE   Antigone   no scorn
don't try to stop me dying with you
and   better late than never   honour
both my brothers thus

ANTIGONE   no   I asked you   you refused Ismene
my solitary death will be enough

ISMENE   how can I live without you ?

ANTIGONE   ask Kreon   your kissy-kissy Uncle
that you love

ISMENE   let me die with you Antigone

ANTIGONE   I'll die   you'll go on   la-la-la-living
            like you chose to

KREON   as mad as each other

ISMENE   how shall I live without her?

KREON   better learn   for she is dead already

ISMENE   you'd execute your own son's bride?

KREON   Haemon will have to find another

ISMENE   he loves Antigone

KREON   but will not marry a traitor I tell you!

ANTIGONE   Haemon   oh Haemon my love
            do you hear how much your father hates you?

KREON   it's not Haemon you love   is it?   it's
                                              Polyneikes

CHORUS   Kreon can you part your own son
            from the one he loves?

KREON   I'm not stopping Haemon's wedding
            death is

CHORUS   then Antigone must die?

KREON   yes

            take them both inside
            don't let them out of your sight
            they might not be so brave   might try to run
            when death approaches

            ANTIGONE *and* ISMENE *are taken away inside.*

CHORUS   fate has fixed on this family
            new disaster is heaped upon old
            for the unhappy house of Laius
            for the cursed children of Oedipus

            some relentless god   perhaps
            pursues them mercilessly
            useless to speculate upon the motives of the gods

            HAEMON *comes.*

CHORUS   here comes Haemon
           your only living son   King Kreon
           how has he taken this?

KREON   it doesn't take a prophet to tell me why you're
                                                        here

           my son   you've heard my sentence
           forget Antigone   your bride not-to-be

           are you still your father's son?   say yes
           Haemon!   that bitch Antigone left me no choice

HAEMON   father I am your son
           no marriage is more important than your good
                                                      opinion
           nor the governance of the wisest parent

KREON   all fathers should have such sons
           and a King would be a laughingstock to all his
                                                        people
           and rightly   who could not even control his own

           I am proud you haven't let
           your former feelings for this Antigone
           blur your judgment
           you are able to put your personal life aside
           as befits the son of a ruler whose interest
           must always lie with the greater and the public
                                                          good

           a fanatic like Antigone would have been no wife
                                                          for you
           believe me   let her marry in hell
           she let them catch her Haemon
           blatant   the only living traitor in all Thebes

           I must keep my oath and execute her
           or I would be a traitor to this city too
           how could I ever stand in judgment on
           citizen or stranger
           if I let Antigone get off scot-free
           just because we were related?
           once you've promised that you're going to do
                                                    something

> better do it   stand by your word
> or no one will obey you in anything   ever
> and   for a king   obedience   in everything
> is all

HAEMON   father
I understand you perfectly

but I'd be a bad son to you
if I didn't put you wise
that not absolutely everyone in Thebes
agrees with you

KREON   meaning what?

HAEMON   only that I hear things
am bound to
that people would never dare to say to you
they're so terrified of you   as is proper

but I'm not the King so I can listen in
to what they're muttering on street corners
or in the shadows

KREON   muttering?

HAEMON   oh   just that they pity her
that she does not deserve to die
that she was absolutely in the right in what she did
that such a sister should be crowned in glory
not rewarded by a vile traitor's death

KREON   I can't break my oath   she dies

HAEMON   if you say so   yes   but father
even a king can change his mind
especially a king

when a torrent sweeps through a forest in a flood
the trees that bend survive
the rigid ones that won't snap off at the root
like rotten teeth   are washed away

you can bend   great minds
are always learning
and someone who's willing to learn and put
                              things right

is far stronger than he who never makes mistakes

KREON   am I to learn wisdom from a boy his age?

HAEMON   I know right from wrong

KREON   and honouring traitors is right?

HAEMON   this one?   yes   that's what the people say

KREON   the people   who cares what the people say
             what kind of king takes orders from the people

HAEMON   a wise one

KREON   in every state   one man makes the laws
             the king

HAEMON   are you a king or are you a tyrant?
             live all alone in an empty city
             if you want to be an absolute ruler

KREON   you're on this woman's side

HAEMON   I'm on no-one's side but this suffering city's

             what Antigone did is not a woman's thing
             but a wholly human thing

KREON   you'll not save her Haemon

HAEMON   then perhaps she won't be the only one to die

KREON   is that a threat?

HAEMON   a promise   unfortunately

KREON   you will regret the day you said that
             stay there   I will show you who is wrong
             and you'll be sorry   bring me Antigone
             bring her to me now
             I will kill her myself
             right here
             right now

HAEMON   never!   stay and watch her die?
             no   never
             nor will you ever see me here again

             go and find some sycophantic scum
             to simper as they watch you play the tinpot tyrant

I have seen and heard enough   excuse me
father   your majesty

HAEMON *storms off angrily, exits.*

CHORUS   Kreon
don't let him storm off like that
at his age despair can be very dangerous

KREON   let him do what he wants
furious or not   despairing or not
he will not save them

CHORUS   what?
no hope for either of them?

KREON   Antigone must die
not Ismene   she's blameless

ONE OF THE CHORUS
but Antigone   how – ?

KREON   she'll be taken up to the mountain
be sealed inside a cave
given food enough for a day or two

it shall not be said Thebes murdered her in cold
blood
I'll not   touch her

once she's in there
she can pray long and hard to her beloved death
the only god she seems to have any respect for
we'll see if her immoderate adoration is requited
death will you love her back?

KREON *exits into palace.*

CHORUS   death   love   love   death
love's the worst of it
poor Haemon
falling that hard for that girl Antigone

duty to a parent?
love will make light of it

love's the worst of it
poor Antigone
loving the dead brother

even more than the living lover

Enter ANTIGONE *walking slowly, her hands bound, with* GUARD.

CHORUS   cry salt tears
to see Antigone
walking towards her death

ANTIGONE   this is my last journey
this sun shining is the sunshine of my last day

death
is walking with me
death
keeping time with my final footsteps as my time
runs out   how it dwindles   oh death doesn't it?
the last of the sand in the glass   tiny grains
                                                    that trickle

death
won't you take me
down where the black water
moans and moves and sucks at the silent shores
                                                    of darkness
oh   will you pull me under

CHORUS   death
dread   death
we fear you as all humans fear you

ANTIGONE   death
won't you dance at my wedding?
death
will you marry me?

CHORUS   death
this maiden courts you and croons to you

ANTIGONE   death
with no-one left to mourn me
death
with no one to miss me
death
with no one to kiss me
kiss me and cover me   drown me
death

CHORUS   Thebes   our home
                home of this maiden
                call her back to you from the dark shores of death

ANTIGONE   this morning I woke up
                to the silence before the battle
                the terror filled silence before
                the terror and the noise of battle
                and I thought of death and of my brothers
                I thought of Eteokles
                I thought of Polyneikes
                waking in the Argive camp among the invaders
                whose armies held our city in a cruel vice
                I thought of the three draughts of poison
                death and my mother had prepared together
                for herself   for Ismene   and for me
                and how   together   we would drink it
                if Polyneikes won

                Ismene came said *sister*
                get up it is your wedding day

                I said   *Ismene I know what day it is*
                today   at last   the battle
                death already has in its greedy maws so many

                Ismene said   *yes many*
                many will die today Antigone
                but it might not be you   might not be me

                get up   your lovely wedding dress
                we must get it ready

                but I knew who I'd marry
                I say yes to you death
                death who takes me still living into my bridal-
                                                        chamber
                that dark cave   takes me virgin into my
                                                        burial-bed
                embraces me
                dear death who has invited all my loved ones
                                                        already
                before me to the feast
                so they'll greet me

this morning I woke up from a dream of life
to the sweet and simple fact of death

Enter KREON *leading* ISMENE. CHORUS
sing urgently to themselves and to KREON *and*
ISMENE.

CHORUS   cry salt tears
to see Antigone
walking towards her death

KREON   weep   wail   mourn   rail
no help for it now

take her away   take her out of my sight

ISMENE *lets out a cry of anguish and collapses
crying out –*

ISMENE   Antigone!

They go off in stately procession, ANTIGONE
and her GUARD. KREON *cries out –*

KREON   I did my best to force her to repent
I pleaded with her to repent
all I asked was she say the word *repentance*

nothing
now it is too late

CHORUS   the girl was stubborn   she went too far
she's cursed
the girl brought this cruel fate upon herself

but we say
cry salt and bitter tears
to see Antigone
walking towards her death

KREON   silence!

The CHORUS *quake, terrified they have gone
too far. Silence, an ominous beat of it, then
enter* TIRESIAS, *his white stick swishing
tapping quicky-quick on the ground.*

TIRESIAS   Thebans
help me

I   blind Tireseas
am searching for Kreon   take me I beg you
straightway to him now

KREON   what is wrong Tiresias?

TIRESIAS   Listen to me now
you are on a knife-edge

listen
I was alone at the altar praying
in my secret   my ancient place of prophecy
then a sound   strange   wild
cacophonous   unholy
suddenly   the sound of birds
screeching   screaming
their great wings beating around my head
wheeling   the noise
the tearing at each other with talons and beaks
the pecking   raucous cries   the bloodied
                                        feathers falling
and suddenly round my feet raged a boiling
                                        pack of dogs
squabbling over carrion
snarling   tearing their prey to bits between
                              them   baying
till   blind as I am   I beat them from the
                                        temple doors

shaking I was   outraged as much as scared
I could not believe the sacrilege
or that the gods could have allowed it
so I prayed
placed my hands on the sacred stone of the altar

I felt blood there   smelled it   saw a vision
dark blood oozing from the torn flesh of a
                                        soldier's corpse
saw the splintered and far-scattered bones
of a human skeleton

KREON   what did this mean?

TIRESIAS   that you   King Kreon
have brought a curse on Thebes

KREON   what curse? how?

TIRESIAS   birds and dogs have defiled our altars
             with the filth of flesh torn from unburied
                                            Polyneikes

             as long as he remains
             unburied   inhuman   some animal offal
             on the earth
             not in it   we can offer nothing
             nothing to the gods they find acceptable

             they are bound to reject even
             our each   our every simplest prayer.

KREON   how can a traitor's fate pollute –?

TIRESIAS   it does
             disgusts them utterly

             Kreon everyone makes mistakes
             but the wise man admits to them
             puts them right

KREON   do you say I am in the wrong?

TIRESIAS   that's right   you let your hatred of Polyniekes
                                            go far too far

             he's dead now so he cannot harm you
             don't try to kill him all over again
             for Thebes' sake

KREON   the target in every state   when things go
                                            wrong's

             the ruler   now even you turn on me Tiresias
             make up portentous stories to spook me

             an outrage to the gods is he? rotting away there
             quietly on the plain?   well
             if the eagles carried strips of him to heaven
             or those dogs sprouted wings and flew up to shit
                                            bits of him
             on the very doorstep of the gods I'd still not
                                            give in

             disgust the gods?   I know
             it's treason and treachery   Tiresias

that disgust them   I know   not
traitors' silly corpses whether strewn or

putrifying

TIRESIAS   can any man think he knows anything?

KREON   more soothsayer gobbledygook
sounds good   means nothing

TIRESIAS   nor do your poor foolish mortal's words

KREON   I am your King

your prophesies are ten a penny
and can be bought for not much more?
who bribed you to say this stuff?

TIRESIAS   bribed me?   paid me?
Tiresias is not to be bought.

KREON   – for I tell you
all the money in the world
will not buy a grave for Polyniekes.

tell your boss you've failed.
you will never make me change my mind

TIRESIAS   I've failed   goodbye

TIRESIAS *begins to exit then wheels round to
deliver.*

but   Kreon   hear me
I swear before this day is over
your son   your Haemon your own
will die to expiate your sins against the dead

die once for that life you sent to a living grave
die once for the corpse of Polyniekes you refused
to honour in a human way

no avoiding of it now
anger is mounting against you
no escape
soon your palace and your city both
will be filled with weeping

TIRESIAS *exits.*

CHORUS   the prophecies of Tiresias are never wrong

KREON   I know
I know it

surely it's wrong to give in?
surer still that what the seer says he sees
scares me to the depths of who I am

Thebans   what do you think I should do?

CHORUS   save this girl
free Antigone   let her bury her brother

KREON   give way?   admit defeat?

CHORUS   hurry
the vengeance of the gods always comes so
swiftly

KREON   it is too hard

CHORUS   but hurry
go
go yourself

ISMENE   take me with you!

CHORUS   don't let anyone else do the dirty work
don't let anyone do it for you

KREON   you're right   yes
I'll go   Ismene come
you'll see I'll save her

where are you Haemon?

follow with axes   soldiers
picks
crowbars
I'll free her

a man must obey his god

Exit KREON *followed by* ISMENE, *both
running.*

CHORUS   Kreon has learned wisdom
there is hope for Thebes and Thebans
the war is over

the war is over
and in a dark cave a frightened girl
does not know love comes running
comes running to her rescue

light in a dark place
forgiveness
a sister's tears of joy
a great King's tears of humility and repentance
forgiveness
light in a dark place

love comes running

Enter ISMENE, *shattered.*

ISMENE   envy Kreon did you?
envy the royal family of the house of Laius?
cursed!

wealth and power
they are nothing   surely you always knew that?

CHORUS   tell   us   what   happened?

ISMENE   I was there   I

saw it all
I was with my uncle Kreon
when we got to the body of Polyniekes
what the dogs had left of it

watched
as he washed the torn and stinking carcass of
                        my brother
I tried to help   he snarled   slapped me off
so I stopped   just stood there

watched   couldn't weep
he said a prayer   I moved my lips
as he honoured Polyneikes my brother with
a sweet   a decent   covering mound of earth

then we went running to Antigone
to the cave where   still living   they interred
                        her
by the time we got there

the wall of stones was all but torn away by
                                        soldiers

we were sure we could hear   something
someone was shouting deep inside   then
                                        silence

slowly
in silence
we walked into the stillness
into the darkness   our torches

Antigone!
Antigone hanging from a rope
my sister   twisted dangling from a
rope fashioned from strips of her own wedding-
                                dress twisted
her slip soaked her trousseau torn
Antigone dangling

Haemon was there he
Haemon howling he
pressed his face to her belly
sobbing
he clutched at her   hugging her
limp lower limbs to him
hanged   Antigone

Antigone
his love   he
pulled out a blade we saw it glinting
he cut the noose   she fell   white   lifeless
broken   he roared
he sprang at his father
spat at his father
spat in his face
his bright dagger at his father's throat

Kreon saw
he stood   would have stood it
would have taken it
accepted it as justice
not lifted a finger
but

Haemon laughed   he turned it
held the blade of the knife towards himself
plunged it
hard into his own body   once

his bursting heart bespattered Antigone
the blood came bubbling
gouts of it   from his loving mouth
as he kissed his Antigone
one last time

and death has heard their vows and married them
for ever

CHORUS   here comes Kreon
Kreon our King   a broken man

KREON   why?

did the gods curse me?
pride   my pride has killed
I am the guilty one
pride   I killed them
I killed the whole future
now all I want to do is die
death come take me   I was wrong

CHORUS   a man who learned
but learned too late

ISMENE   why should death do you any favours?
why should death spare you
a long and miserable life?

here stands Ismene
who once upon a time loved life
but now
how could it be otherwise?
longs for nothing more   or less   than death

suffered enough?
who says so?   unless the gods do
Kreon we cannot die

here stands Ismene
sister of Antigone
in a sea of death condemned to life

CHORUS   it seems we are survivors too   thus far
          Thebans   in a city that's still standing
          thus far   we'd like to hope we've seen it all
          until the day we die we cannot say
          Thebans we have come through the worst of it

          the house of Laius is destroyed
          love is dead in Thebes
          Kreon's pride punished
          if there are gods we fear them
          as much as we fear a godless universe
          horror gags us
          when we should have spoken out we were silent
          kept our heads down survived   thus far

          cities stand so tall
          we live in them forgetting they can be broken
          brought down in flaking ashes
          smoke and horror
          dust

          The End.

A Nick Hern Book

Thebans first published in Great Britain in 2003
as a paperback original by Nick Hern Books Limited,
14 Larden Road, London W3 7ST, in association with
Theatre Babel, Glasgow

Typeset by Country Setting, Kingsdown, Kent CT14 8ES
Printed by Bookmarque, Croydon, Surrey

ISBN 1 85459 757 4

A CIP catalogue record for this book is available from
the British Library